Archery

by Julie Murray

Abdo
ARTISTIC SPORTS
Kids

Abdo Kids Jumbo is an Imprint of Abdo Kids
abdobooks.com

abdobooks.com

Published by Abdo Kids, a division of ABDO, P.O. Box 398166, Minneapolis, Minnesota 55439. Copyright © 2023 by Abdo Consulting Group, Inc. International copyrights reserved in all countries. No part of this book may be reproduced in any form without written permission from the publisher. Abdo Kids Jumbo™ is a trademark and logo of Abdo Kids.

Printed in the United States of America, North Mankato, Minnesota.

102022

012023

 THIS BOOK CONTAINS RECYCLED MATERIALS

Photo Credits: Getty Images, Shutterstock

Production Contributors: Teddy Borth, Jennie Forsberg, Grace Hansen
Design Contributors: Candice Keimig, Pakou Moua

Library of Congress Control Number: 2022937167
Publisher's Cataloging-in-Publication Data

Names: Murray, Julie, author.

Title: Archery / by Julie Murray

Description: Minneapolis, Minnesota : Abdo Kids, 2023 | Series: Artistic sports | Includes online resources and index.

Identifiers: ISBN 9781098264192 (lib. bdg.) | ISBN 9781098264758 (ebook) | ISBN 9781098265038 (Read-to-Me ebook)

Subjects: LCSH: Archery--Juvenile literature. | Bow and arrow--Juvenile literature. | Archery--Rules--Juvenile literature. | Sports--Juvenile literature. | Sports--History--Juvenile literature.

Classification: DDC 799.32--dc23

Table of Contents

Archery 4

Bows and Arrows 8

Shooting 14

Types of Archery 16

More Facts 22

Glossary 23

Index 24

Abdo Kids Code 24

Archery

Archery is a sport that uses a bow and arrows. The first known archers were ancient Egyptians who lived about 12,000 years ago. Then, archery skills were used in **combat** and to hunt.

5

Today, archery is a **competitive** sport. Some hunters still use a bow and arrow. Archery can also be a **hobby**.

7

Bows and Arrows

A bow and arrow are the main equipment used in archery. There are different types of each. The kind being used depends on what type of archery is being performed.

A bow has a string attached to upper and lower limbs. There is a grip and arrow rest between the limbs. Some bows are used by pulling and releasing the string by hand. Others have a **mechanism** to release the string.

bow string —— upper limb

lower limb

An arrow has a tip, shaft, nock, and fletchings. The nock holds the bowstring. The fletchings **stabilize** the arrow in flight.

Shooting

To shoot an arrow, the body should be **perpendicular** to the target. The bowstring is placed in the nock. The bow is extended out. The string is drawn back. The archer aims at the target and releases the arrow.

Types of Archery

Target archery is the most popular type. It can be done indoors or outdoors. Archers shoot at large targets that are set at varying distances.

Field archery is done on an outdoor course. Archers shoot at targets set at different distances and heights along a trail.

Outdoor trails and woods are where 3D archery takes place. Archers shoot at three-dimensional targets that look like animals.

More Facts

- A person who is an expert at archery is called a marksman. Someone who loves archery is called a toxophilite.

- The bag that is used to hold arrows is called a quiver.

- Women were first allowed to compete in archery at the 1904 Olympic games. It was the only Olympic sport that allowed women to compete that year.

Glossary

combat – fighting, especially against an enemy in war.

competitive – having to do with or decided by competition.

hobby – an interest or activity that one does for pleasure in one's spare time.

mechanism – the working or moving part or process that causes a result.

perpendicular – at a right angle to.

stabilize – to make firm, steady, or stable.

Index

ancient Egyptians 4

archer 4, 14, 16, 18, 20

arrows 4, 6, 8, 10, 12, 14

bow 4, 6, 8, 10, 12, 14

bowstring 10, 12, 14

competition 6

field archery 18

fletching 12

hobby 6

hunting 4, 6

method 10, 14

nock 12, 14

target 14, 16, 18, 20

target archery 16

3D archery 20

Visit **abdokids.com** to access crafts, games, videos, and more!

Use Abdo Kids code **AAK4192** or scan this QR code!

24